United States General Accounting Office

GAO

Report to the Subcommittee on
Government Efficiency, Financial
Management and Intergovernmental
Relations, Committee on Government
Reform, House of Representatives

May 2002

INFORMATION SECURITY

Additional Actions Needed to Fully Implement Reform Legislation

Accountability ★ Integrity ★ Reliability

GAO-02-407

United States General Accounting Office
Washington, D.C. 20548

May 2, 2002

The Honorable Stephen Horn
Chairman, Subcommittee on Government Efficiency, Financial
Management and Intergovernmental Relations
Committee on Government Reform
House of Representatives

The Honorable Janice Schakowsky
Ranking Minority Member
Subcommittee on Government Efficiency, Financial Management and
Intergovernmental Relations
Committee on Government Reform
House of Representatives

In March, we testified before your subcommittee on the federal
government's first-year efforts to implement legislative provisions for
Government Information Security Reform (the reform provisions).[1] In
brief, we reported that initial implementation of the reform provisions is a
significant step in improving federal agencies' information security
programs and addressing their serious, pervasive information security
weaknesses, and has resulted in agency benefits and important actions by
the administration to address information security.

We also noted that additional actions by the Office of Management and
Budget (OMB) are needed to (1) further guide agencies and encourage
them to implement the reform provision requirements and (2) provide the
Congress with the information it needs for overseeing agencies'
implementation, compliance, and corrective action efforts, as well as for its
related budget deliberations. Such actions should be taken immediately to
assist the agencies in their second-year effort to implement the reform
provisions and to aid the Congress in considering legislation to extend the
reform provision requirements beyond their original 2-year authorization.[2]

---

[1]U.S. General Accounting Office, *Information Security: Additional Actions Needed to
Fully Implement Reform Provisions*, GAO-02-470T (Washington, D.C.: Mar. 6, 2002).

[2]The reform provisions were enacted as Title X, Subtitle G—Government Information
Security Reform, Floyd D. Spence National Defense Authorization Act for Fiscal Year 2001,
P.L. 106-398, October 30, 2000. These provisions became effective November 29, 2000, and
are in effect for 2 years after this date.

To help ensure that these actions are taken, we are making recommendations to OMB based on the suggestions and issues raised in our March 2002 testimony for which we have not previously made recommendations. This testimony is reprinted in appendix I. We performed our work from May 2001 through March 2002 in accordance with generally accepted government auditing standards. OMB provided us with comments on a draft of this report, which are discussed in the "Agency Comments" section.

Recommendations

To facilitate more efficient and effective agency management of and reporting on the implementation of information security requirements of the reform provisions, we recommend that the director of the Office of Management and Budget direct his staff to provide additional guidance on

- appropriate performance measures to enable the agencies to better determine and report their progress in implementing the security requirements;

- more specific definitions and examples of information-security-related costs to enable the agencies to more consistently identify, track, and report these costs; and

- a more detailed description of the required scope of the annual management reviews regarding the extent to which (1) systems must be reviewed annually and (2) security controls must be tested and evaluated as part of this review process.

To enhance oversight of federal information security by the Congress and its related budget deliberations, we further recommend that the director of the Office of Management and Budget

- authorize the heads of federal departments and agencies to release information from their corrective action plans to the Congress and GAO that would (1) identify specific weaknesses to be addressed, their relative priority, the actions to be taken, and the timeframes for completing these actions and (2) provide their quarterly updates on the status of completing these actions;

- provide the Congress with appropriate summary information on the results of the audits of the evaluations for information security programs for national security systems; and

- in addition to the information currently reported, explicitly identify in future OMB annual reports to the Congress, the overall status of agencies' efforts to implement each of the information security program requirements specified by the reform provisions.

In addition, to help ensure that annual independent evaluations appropriately consider all agency systems as intended by the reform provisions, we also recommend that director of the Office of Management and Budget, through its budgetary and reform provision oversight responsibilities, encourage agencies' inspectors general to

- appropriately consider both financial and nonfinancial systems in selecting the subset of systems for testing information security control techniques during their annual independent evaluations,

- provide an independent assessment of agencies' corrective action plans in their future evaluations, and

- obtain appropriate resources to support these evaluations and their other information security audit needs.

Agency Comments

OMB's Chief of the Information Policy and Technology Branch, Office of Information and Regulatory Affairs, provided us with oral comments on a draft of this report. Emphasizing that comments pertain specifically to our recommendations, the OMB chief generally concurred with the recommendations and advised that OMB and the agencies identified similar areas for improvement and have drafted revised fiscal year 2002 reporting guidance that would address the recommendations as appropriate.

The OMB chief also wanted to clarify several key issues related to our recommendations on providing to the Congress information on agencies corrective action plans, reporting to the Congress on the status of agencies' efforts to implement information security program requirements, and the implementation of our recommendations within the context of OMB's statutory roles and responsibilities. The OMB chief noted that he recognizes Congress's oversight role regarding agencies' actions to correct information security weaknesses, and at this time, OMB is continuing to develop a solution for next year's reporting to provide to the Congress information on agencies' corrective actions. However, he emphasized that since OMB's objective is to maintain the confidentiality of predecisional information contained in agencies' corrective action plans and that he believed removing such information from current year plans would be difficult, OMB is not having the agencies prepare information on their current plans that would be releasable to the Congress.

The OMB chief was also concerned about whether the reform provisions require OMB to specifically report to the Congress on the implementation of each of the law's information security program requirements. He believed that such detailed reporting conflicts with OMB's focus on overall information security program management. Finally, in discussing implementation of other recommendations regarding reporting information to the Congress on national security systems and encouraging actions by inspectors general, the OMB chief asked that his comments indicate that in doing so, OMB remains cognizant of (1) its statutory role and responsibilities related to national security systems and (2) the statutory independence of the inspectors general.

Regarding OMB's position on providing information on agencies' corrective action plans to the Congress, we believe that the lack of such important information for this year's plans would delay Congress' consideration of agencies' corrective actions in its oversight and budget deliberations for federal information security for another year. We will continue to work with OMB in an effort to find workable solutions to obtain this important information from these first-year plans, as well as from future agency corrective action plans. Regarding OMB's concern about reporting to the Congress on agencies' progress in implementing each information security program requirement, the reform provisions require OMB to report to the Congress each year on the results of the agencies' independent evaluations. These evaluations are required to include an assessment (made on the basis of testing) of the requirements of this law, which include specific requirements for an agencywide information security program. OMB's report to the Congress this year provided much useful information, but did not summarize the status of agencies' efforts to implement all requirements of an information security program, such as agencies' progress in conducting risk assessments. Thus, we continue to believe that OMB's report to the Congress should include the status of agencies' efforts to implement each of the reform provisions' information security program requirements.

We are sending copies of this report to the chairmen and ranking minority members of the Senate and House Committees on Appropriations, the Senate and House Budget Committees, Senate Committee on

Governmental Affairs, the House Committee on Government Reform and its Subcommittee on Technology and Procurement Policy, and the House Committee on Energy and Commerce. We are also sending copies of this report to the director of the Office of Management and Budget. Copies will also be made available to others upon request.

Should you or your staff have any questions concerning this report, please call me at (202) 512-3317 or Ben Ritt, assistant director, at (202) 512-6443. We can also be reached by e-mail at daceyr@gao.gov and rittw@gao.gov, respectively. Key contributors to this assignment are listed in appendix II.

Robert F. Dacey
Director, Information Security Issues

United States General Accounting Office

GAO

Testimony

Before the Subcommittee on Government Efficiency,
Financial Management and Intergovernmental Relations,
Committee on Government Reform, House of
Representatives

For Release on Delivery
Expected at
10 a.m. EST
Wednesday,
March 6, 2002

INFORMATION SECURITY

Additional Actions Needed to Fully Implement Reform Legislation

Statement of Robert F. Dacey
Director, Information Security Issues

GAO-02-470T

Mr. Chairman and Members of the Subcommittee:

I am pleased to be here today to discuss efforts by the federal government to implement provisions for Government Information Security Reform (the reform provisions) that were enacted as part of the National Defense Authorization Act for Fiscal Year 2001.[1] Federal agencies rely extensively on computerized systems and electronic data to support their missions and critical operations. Concerned with reports that continuing, pervasive security weaknesses place federal operations at significant risk of disruption, tampering, fraud, and inappropriate disclosures of sensitive information, the Congress enacted the reform provisions to reduce these risks and provide more effective oversight of federal information security.

In my testimony today, I will first describe some of the improvement efforts and benefits that have resulted from this first year implementation of the reform provisions. Next, I will describe the results of our evaluation of actions by the Office of Management and Budget (OMB), 24 of the largest federal agencies, and these agencies' inspectors general (IGs) to implement the reform provisions. As part of this discussion, I will also summarize the overall results of these actions and, in particular, note any challenges to effective implementation or oversight of the reform provisions.

Mr. Chairman, as you know we have been conducting a review of the implementation of the reform provisions for you and the ranking member. Today, I will provide the preliminary results of our review. In conducting this review, we interviewed officials and staff in the offices of the chief information officer (CIO) and the IGs for 24 of the largest federal agencies. We reviewed OMB guidance and instructions related to the reform provisions and, for the 24 agencies, analyzed summaries of their management reviews of their information security programs. Further, we analyzed the IGs' summaries and reports on their independent evaluations of the agencies' information security programs. We also analyzed OMB's fiscal year 2001 report to the Congress on the results of these reviews and evaluations.[2]

---

[1] Title X, Subtitle G—Government Information Security Reform, Floyd D. Spence National Defense Authorization Act for Fiscal Year 2001, P.L. 106-398, October 30, 2000.

[2] Office of Management and Budget, *FY 2001 Report to Congress on Federal Government Information Security Reform*, February 2002.

We performed this review from May 2001 to March 2002 in accordance
with generally accepted government auditing standards.

Background

Dramatic increases in computer interconnectivity, especially in the use of
the Internet, continue to revolutionize the way our government, our
nation, and much of the world communicate and conduct business.
However, this widespread interconnectivity also poses significant risks to
our computer systems and, more important, to the critical operations and
infrastructures they support, such as telecommunications, power
distribution, public health, national defense (including the military's
warfighting capability), law enforcement, government, and emergency
services. Likewise, the speed and accessibility that create the enormous
benefits of the computer age, if not properly controlled, allow individuals
and organizations to inexpensively eavesdrop on or interfere with these
operations from remote locations for mischievous or malicious purposes,
including fraud or sabotage.

As greater amounts of money are transferred through computer systems,
as more sensitive economic and commercial information is exchanged
electronically, and as the nation's defense and intelligence communities
increasingly rely on commercially available information technology, the
likelihood increases that information attacks will threaten vital national
interests. Further, the events of September 11, 2001, underscored the need
to protect America's cyberspace against potentially disastrous cyber
attacks—attacks that could also be coordinated to coincide with physical
terrorist attacks to maximize the impact of both.

Since September 1996, we have reported that poor information security is
a widespread federal problem with potentially devastating consequences.[3]
Although agencies have taken steps to redesign and strengthen their
information system security programs, our analyses of information
security at major federal agencies have shown that federal systems were
not being adequately protected from computer-based threats, even though
these systems process, store, and transmit enormous amounts of sensitive
data and are indispensable to many federal agency operations. In addition,
in both 1998 and 2000, we analyzed audit results for 24 of the largest
federal agencies and found that all 24 had significant information security

---

[3]U.S. General Accounting Office, *Information Security: Opportunities for Improved OMB
Oversight of Agency Practices*. GAO/AIMD-96-110. Washington, D.C.: September 24, 1996.

weaknesses.[4] As a result of these analyses, we have identified information security as a governmentwide high-risk issue in reports to the Congress since 1997—most recently in January 2001.[5]

To fully understand the significance of the weaknesses we identified, it is necessary to link them to the risks they present to federal operations and assets. Virtually all federal operations are supported by automated systems and electronic data, and agencies would find it difficult, if not impossible, to carry out their missions and account for their resources without these information assets. Hence, the degree of risk caused by security weaknesses is extremely high.

The weaknesses identified place a broad array of federal operations and assets at risk. For example,

- resources, such as federal payments and collections, could be lost or stolen;
- computer resources could be used for unauthorized purposes or to launch attacks on others;
- sensitive information, such as taxpayer data, social security records, medical records, and proprietary business information, could be inappropriately disclosed or browsed or copied for purposes of espionage or other types of crime;
- critical operations, such as those supporting national defense and emergency services, could be disrupted;
- data could be modified or destroyed for purposes of fraud or disruption; and
- agency missions could be undermined by embarrassing incidents that result in diminished confidence in their ability to conduct operations and fulfill their fiduciary responsibilities.

U.S. General Accounting Office, *Information Security: Serious Weaknesses Place Critical Federal Operations and Assets at Risk.* GAO/AIMD-98-92. Washington, D.C.: September 23, 1998; *Information Security: Serious and Widespread Weaknesses Persist at Federal Agencies.* GAO/AIMD-00-295. Washington, D.C.: September 6, 2000.

[5]U.S. General Accounting Office, *High-Risk Series: Information Management and Technology.* GAO/HR-97-9. Washington, D.C.: February 1, 1997; *High-Risk Series: An Update.* GAO/HR-99-1. Washington, D.C.: January 1999; *High Risk Series: An Update.* GAO-01-263. Washington, D.C.: January 2001.

Page 3   GAO-02-470T

Concerned with accounts of attacks on commercial systems via the Internet and reports of significant weaknesses in federal computer systems that make them vulnerable to attack, on October 30, 2000, Congress enacted Government Information Security Reform provisions as part of the Floyd D. Spence National Defense Authorization Act for Fiscal Year 2001. These provisions became effective November 29, 2000, and are in effect for 2 years after this date. The reform provisions supplement information security requirements established in the Computer Security Act of 1987, the Paperwork Reduction Act of 1995, and the Clinger-Cohen Act of 1996 and are consistent with existing information security guidance issued by OMB[6] and the National Institute of Standards and Technology (NIST),[7] as well as audit and best practice guidance issued by GAO.[8] Most importantly, however, the provisions consolidate these separate requirements and guidance into an overall framework for managing information security and establish new annual review, independent evaluation, and reporting requirements to help ensure agency implementation and both OMB and congressional oversight.

The legislation assigned specific responsibilities to OMB, agency heads and CIOs, and the IGs. OMB is responsible for establishing and overseeing policies, standards and guidelines for information security. This includes the authority to approve agency information security programs, but delegates OMB's responsibilities with regard to national security systems to national security agencies. OMB is also required to submit an annual report to the Congress summarizing results of agencies' evaluations of their information security programs. The reform provisions do not specify a date for this report.

Each agency, including national security agencies, is to establish an agencywide risk-based information security program to be overseen by the agency CIO and ensure that information security is practiced throughout

---

[6]Primarily OMB Circular A-130, Appendix III, "Security of Federal Automated Information Resources," February 1996.

[7]Numerous publications made available at http://www.itl.nist.gov/ including National Institute of Standards and Technology, *Generally Accepted Principles and Practices for Securing Information Technology Systems*, NIST Special Publication 800-14, September 1996.

[8]U.S. General Accounting Office, *Federal Information System Controls Manual, Volume 1—Financial Statement Audits*. GAO/AIMD-12.19.6. Washington, D.C.: January 1999; *Information Security Management: Learning from Leading Organizations*. GAO/AIMD-98-68. Washington, D.C.: May 1998.

the life cycle of each agency system. Specifically, this program is to
include

- periodic risk assessments that consider internal and external threats to the integrity, confidentiality, and availability of systems, and to data supporting critical operations and assets;
- the development and implementation of risk-based, cost-effective policies and procedures to provide security protections for information collected or maintained by or for the agency;
- training on security responsibilities for information security personnel and on security awareness for agency personnel;
- periodic management testing and evaluation of the effectiveness of policies, procedures, controls, and techniques;
- a process for identifying and remediating any significant deficiencies;
- procedures for detecting, reporting and responding to security incidents; and
- an annual program review by agency program officials.

In addition to the responsibilities listed above, the reform provisions require each agency to have an annual independent evaluation of its information security program and practices, including control testing and compliance assessment. The evaluations of non-national-security systems are to be performed by the agency IG or an independent evaluator, and the results of these evaluations are to be reported to OMB. For the evaluation of national security systems, special provisions include designation of evaluators by national security agencies, restricted reporting of evaluation results, and an audit of the independent evaluation performed by the IG or an independent evaluator. For national security systems, only the results of each audit of an evaluation are to be reported to OMB.

Finally, the reform provisions also assign additional responsibilities for information security policies, standards, guidance, training, and other functions to other agencies. These agencies are NIST, the Department of Defense, the Intelligence Community, the Attorney General, the General Services Administration (GSA), and the Office of Personnel Management.

With oversight jurisdiction for information security, this subcommittee has continued to hold hearings on the status of information security in the federal government. Most recently, on November 9, 2001, the subcommittee issued information security "grades" based primarily on the

Page 5   GAO-02-470T

agencies' reform provision review summaries and IG evaluations that were submitted to OMB. The overall grade for the federal government was an "F."

Results in Brief

The initial implementation of the reform provisions is a significant step in improving federal agencies' information security programs and addressing their serious, pervasive information security weaknesses. The legislation consolidates information security requirements into an overall management framework covering all agency systems, adds new statutory evaluation and reporting requirements that facilitate implementation of these requirements, and strengthens OMB and congressional oversight. Agencies have noted benefits of this first-year implementation, including increased management attention to and accountability for information security. In addition, the legislation has resulted in other important actions by the administration to address information security, such as plans to integrate information security into the President's Management Agenda Scorecard.

OMB is using a combination of formal guidance, review and analysis of agency-reported material, agency discussion and feedback, and monitoring of corrective actions to oversee and coordinate agency compliance with the requirements of the reform provisions. This oversight contributed to agency implementation and reporting efforts. However, further guidance is needed to ensure that agencies effectively implement these requirements and can show their progress in these efforts. For example, OMB's reporting guidance required agencies to identify performance measures and actual performance for implementing key security requirements like assessing risk and testing and evaluating security controls, but did not provide guidance on establishing such measures. Thus, agencies were left to independently develop their own measures.

In February 2002, OMB released its required annual report to the Congress on the results of agency evaluations. In this report, OMB commended agencies' improvement efforts, but noted that many agencies have significant deficiencies in every important area of security. OMB also identified a number of common agency security weaknesses, including a lack of senior management attention, inadequate accountability for job and program performance, and a limited capability to detect vulnerabilities or intrusions. Although OMB's report provides an overview of agencies' progress and status, the report does not specifically address several requirements of the reform provisions, including the adequacy of agencies' corrective action plans and the results of evaluations for national security systems. Further, OMB considers some agency material, such as agencies' corrective action plans, to contain predecisional budget information and will not authorize agencies to release this material to the Congress or GAO. The lack of such important information limits congressional oversight of agencies' implementation, compliance, and corrective action efforts, as well as for budget deliberations. We plan to continue working with OMB in an effort to find workable solutions to obtain the information needed for congressional oversight.

In response to the reform provisions, agencies reviewed their information security programs, reported the results of these reviews to OMB, and developed plans to correct identified weaknesses. However, their reviews showed that agencies have not established information security programs consistent with the legislative requirements and that significant weaknesses exist. Although agency actions are now underway to strengthen information security and implement these requirements, significant improvement will require sustained management attention and OMB and congressional oversight.

The IGs also played a critical role in this process by independently evaluating the agencies' implementation efforts and verifying the effectiveness of security controls. However, the IGs' first-year efforts to evaluate agency information security were largely based on existing or ongoing audit work to evaluate agency information security, which in a number of instances, consisted primarily of audits of financial systems. While their future evaluations should expand to include more systems supporting nonfinancial operations, the IGs' first-year evaluations helped identify significant weaknesses in all 24 of the largest federal agencies—weaknesses that were not always identified by the agencies in their reports.

Given recent events and reports that critical operations and assets are highly vulnerable to cyber attack, it is essential that the Congress have adequate information to oversee and fund federal information security efforts and that these efforts be guided by a comprehensive strategy for improvement. OMB should, therefore, consider providing the Congress with additional information that the agencies submitted under the reform provisions, such as appropriate information from the agencies' corrective action plans. In addition, there are a number of important steps that the administration and the agencies should take to ensure that information security receives appropriate attention and resources and that known deficiencies are addressed, including delineating the roles and responsibilities of the numerous entities involved in federal information security and related aspects of critical infrastructure protection, providing more specific guidance to agencies on the security controls that they need to implement, and allocating sufficient agency resources for information security.

Reform Provisions Increase Management Attention to Information Security

The initial implementation of the reform provisions is a significant step in addressing the serious, pervasive weaknesses in the federal government's information security. The legislation consolidates existing security requirements and adds new statutory requirements designed to improve information security, such as independent evaluations and annual reporting. In addition, implementation of the provisions has improved agency focus on information security and resulted in important actions by the administration.

Although security requirements existed in law and policy before this law, the reform provisions put into law several important additional requirements. First, the provisions require a risk-based security management program covering all operations and assets of the agency and those provided or managed for the agency by others to be implemented by agency program managers and CIOs. Instituting such an approach is important since many agencies had not effectively evaluated their information security risks and implemented appropriate controls. Our studies of public and private best practices have shown that effective security program management requires implementing a process that provides for a cycle of risk management activities as now included in the reform provisions.[9] Moreover, other efforts to improve agency information security will not be fully effective and lasting unless they are supported by a strong agencywide security management program.

Second, the reform provisions require an annual independent evaluation of each agency's information security program. Individually, as well as collectively, these evaluations can provide much needed information for improved oversight by OMB and the Congress. Our years of auditing agency security programs have shown that independent tests and evaluations are essential to verifying the effectiveness of computer-based controls. Audits can also evaluate agency implementation of management

---

[9]U.S. General Accounting Office, *Information Security Management: Learning from Leading Organizations.* GAO/AIMD-98-68. Washington, D.C.: May 1998; *Information Security Risk Management: Practices of Leading Organizations.* GAO/AIMD-00-33. Washington, D.C.: November 1999.

initiatives, thus promoting management accountability. Annual independent evaluations of agency information security programs will help drive reform because they will spotlight both the obstacles and progress toward improving information security and provide a means of measuring progress, much like the financial statement audits required by the Government Management Reform Act of 1994. Further, independent reviews proved to be an important mechanism for monitoring progress and uncovering problems that needed attention in the federal government's efforts to meet the Year 2000 computing challenge.

Third, the reform provisions take a governmentwide approach to information security by accommodating a wide range of information security needs and applying requirements to all agencies, including those engaged in national security. This is important because the information security needs of civilian agency operations and those of national security operations have converged in recent years. In the past, when sensitive information was more likely to be maintained on paper or in stand-alone computers, the main concern was data confidentiality, especially as it pertained to classified national security data. Now, virtually all agencies rely on interconnected computers to maintain information and carry out operations that are essential to their missions. While the confidentiality needs of these data vary, all agencies must be concerned about the integrity and the availability of their systems and data. It is important for all agencies to understand these various types of risks and take appropriate steps to manage them.

Fourth, the annual reporting requirements provide a means for both OMB and the Congress to oversee the effectiveness of agency and government-wide information security, measure progress in improving information security, and consider information security in budget deliberations. In addition to management reviews, annual IG reporting of the independent evaluation results to OMB and OMB's reporting of these results to the Congress provide the Congress with an objective assessment of agencies' information security programs on which to base its oversight and budgeting activities. This reporting also facilitates a process to help ensure consistent identification of information security weaknesses by both the IG and agency management.

In addition to new statutory provisions, first-year implementation of the reform provisions has yielded significant benefits in terms of agency focus on information security. A number of agencies stated that as a result of implementing the reform provisions, they are taking significant steps to

Page 9   GAO-02-470T

improve their information security programs. For example, one agency
stated that the legislation provided it with the opportunity to identify some
systemic program-level weaknesses for which it plans to undertake
separate initiatives targeted specifically to improve the weaknesses. Other
benefits agencies observed included (1) higher visibility of information
security within the agencies, (2) increased awareness of information
security requirements among department personnel, (3) recognition that
program managers are to be held accountable for the security of their
operations, (4) greater agency consideration of security throughout the
system life cycle, and (5) justification for additional resources and funding
needed to improve security. Agency IGs also viewed the reform provisions
as a positive step towards improving information security particularly by
increasing agency management's focus on this issue.

Implementation of the reform provisions has also resulted in important
actions by the administration, which if properly implemented, should
continue to improve information security in the federal government. For
example, OMB has issued guidance that information technology
investments will not be funded unless security is incorporated into and
funded as part of each investment, and NIST has established a Computer
Security Expert Assist Team to review agencies' computer security
management. The administration also has plans to

- direct all large agencies to undertake a review to identify and prioritize
  critical assets within the agencies and their interrelationships with other
  agencies and the private sector, as well as a cross-government review to
  ensure that all critical government processes and assets have been
  identified;
- integrate security into the President's Management Agenda Scorecard;
- develop workable measures of performance;
- develop e-training on mandatory topics, including security; and
- explore methods to disseminate vulnerability patches to agencies more
  effectively.

OMB has Guided and Overseen Agency Implementation

On January 16, 2001, OMB issued guidance to the agencies on implementing the reform provisions that summarized OMB, agency, and IG responsibilities, and provided answers to other specific implementation questions.[10] OMB followed up the implementation guidance with agency reporting instructions first issued in draft form in April and then in final form on June 22.[11] These final reporting instructions directed agencies to transmit copies of the annual agency program reviews, IG independent evaluations, and for national security systems, audits of the independent evaluations to OMB 3 months later, on September 10, 2001—the same time they were to submit their fiscal year 2003 budget materials. In addition to the program reviews and evaluations, agency heads were also to provide a brief executive summary developed by the agency CIO, agency program officials, and the IG based on the results of their work.

The OMB reporting instructions also listed specific topics that the agencies were to address, many of which were referenced back to corresponding requirements of the reform provisions. These topics, which became the basic structure of the executive summaries submitted by the agencies and most IGs, basically asked that agencies identify, describe, or report:

1. Total security funding as found in the agency's fiscal year 2001 budget request, fiscal year 2001 budget enacted, and the fiscal year 2002 budget request.
2. The total number of programs included in the program reviews or independent evaluations.
3. The methods used to conduct the program reviews and independent evaluations.
4. Any material weakness in policies, procedures, or practices as identified and required to be reported under existing law.
5. The specific measures and actual performance for performance measures that agencies used to ensure that for operations and assets under their

---

[10]"Guidance on Implementing the Government Information Security Reform Act," Memorandum for the Heads of Executive Departments and Agencies, Jack Lew, Director, M-01-08, January 16, 2001.

[11]"Reporting Instructions for the Government Information Security Reform Act," Memorandum for the Heads of Executive Departments and Agencies, Mitchell E. Daniels, Jr., Director, M-01-24, June 22, 2001.

control, agency program officials have assessed the risk, determined the appropriate level of security, maintained an up-to-date security plan (that is practiced throughout the life cycle) for each supporting system, and tested and evaluated security controls and techniques.

6. The specific measures and actual performance for performance measures that agencies used to ensure that the agency CIO (a) adequately maintains an agencywide security program, (b) ensures the effective implementation of the program and evaluates the performance of major agency components, and (c) ensures that agency employees with significant security responsibilities are trained.

7. How the agency ensures that employees are sufficiently trained in their security responsibilities to include identifying the total number of agency employees, the types of security training available during the reporting period, the number of agency employees that received each type of training, and the total costs of providing such training.

8. The agency's documented procedures for reporting security incidents and sharing information regarding common vulnerabilities.

9. How the agency integrates security into its capital planning and investment control process.

10. The specific methodology and how it has been implemented by the agency to identify, prioritize, and protect critical assets within its enterprise architecture, including links with key external systems.

11. The specific measures and actual performance for performance measures that the head of the agency used to ensure that the agency's information security plan is practiced throughout the life cycle of each agency system.

12. How the agency has integrated its information and information technology security program with its critical infrastructure protection responsibilities and other security programs.

13. The specific methods used by the agency to ensure that contractor-provided services or services provided by another agency are adequately secure and meet the requirements of the reform provisions and other governmentwide and agency policy and guidance.

The reporting instructions also included an additional requirement for each agency head to work with the CIO and program officials to provide a strategy to correct security weaknesses identified through the annual program reviews, independent evaluations, other reviews or audits performed throughout the reporting period, as well as any uncompleted actions identified before the reporting period. Due to OMB by October 31, 2001, this information was to include a "plan of action and milestones" (corrective action plan) that listed the weaknesses; showed required

Page 12   GAO-02-470T

resources, milestones, and completion dates; and described how the agency planned to address these weaknesses. In response to agency requests, on October 17, OMB provided more detailed guidance for preparing and submitting these corrective action plans, which also provided a sample spreadsheet-type format.[12] The guidance also established a requirement for agencies to submit quarterly status updates to OMB with the first update due on January 31, 2002.

OMB's guidance addressed many key information security requirements in the reform provisions, and agencies generally considered the guidance beneficial in summarizing their efforts to implement these requirements. However, with their reports due to OMB on September 10, several agencies questioned the timeliness of the final reporting guidance being issued less than 3 months before this deadline.

Several agencies also noted the need for additional clarification or guidance in some areas. For example, our analysis of agency executive summaries showed that many agencies did not have or were still in the process of developing and implementing security performance measures. Some thought additional guidance on appropriate measures would be helpful and more cost-effective than having each agency develop its own. Other agencies had questions regarding what should be identified and reported as security costs in their budgets.

In addition to providing guidance, OMB also reviewed the results of agencies' program reviews and independent evaluations and consulted with officials in the agencies to clarify information and provide feedback. OMB also sent letters to the agency heads that provided the results of its assessment of the agencies' submissions for the reform provisions and either conditionally approved or disapproved their information security programs. Further, OMB states in its report to the Congress that it will discuss security corrective action plans with each agency and monitor their progress through the quarterly updates that agencies are to submit. These actions should contribute to OMB's effective oversight and help focus agencies' improvement efforts. However, OMB's sustained commitment to both implementing the reform provisions and overseeing

---

[12]"Guidance for Preparing and Submitting Security Plans of Action and Milestones," Memorandum for the Heads of Executive Departments and Agencies, Mitchell E. Daniels, Jr., Director, M-02-01, October 17, 2001.

Page 13   GAO-02-470T

agencies will be critical to ensuring that agencies substantially improve
their information security programs.

Key Information Needed for Congressional Oversight

On February 13, 2002, OMB released its required report to the Congress to
summarize the agency independent evaluations. Based on reports from
over 50 departments and agencies and focusing on management issues as
opposed to technical or operational issues, this report (1) provides an
overview of OMB and agencies' implementation efforts; (2) summarizes
the overall results of OMB's analyses; (3) includes individual agency
summaries for the 24 of the largest federal departments and agencies; and
(4) includes brief summary remarks for small and independent agencies.
OMB notes that although examples of good security exist in many
agencies, and others are working very hard to improve their performance,
many agencies have significant deficiencies in every important area of
security. In particular, the report highlights six common security
weaknesses:

- a lack of senior management attention to information security;
- inadequate accountability for job and program performance related to
  information technology security;
- limited security training for general users, information technology
  professionals, and security professionals;
- inadequate integration of security into the capital planning and investment
  control process;
- poor security for contractor-provided services; and
- limited capability to detect, report, and share information on
  vulnerabilities or to detect intrusions, suspected intrusions, or virus
  infections.

Overall, OMB views its report to the Congress and the agency reports to be
a valuable baseline to record agency security performance—a baseline
captured with more detailed information than previously available that
will be useful for oversight by agencies, IGs, OMB, GAO, and the Congress.

While we agree and believe that OMB's report provides a useful overview
of OMB and agency efforts to comply with the reform provisions, certain
additional information not included in the report is necessary to fully
assess and oversee these efforts. The lack of such important information
limits congressional oversight for agencies' implementation, compliance,

and corrective action efforts, as well as for budget deliberations. Specifically, OMB's report does not address the following:

- The report does not provide any specific analysis or opinion on the adequacy of agency corrective action plans that were submitted to OMB in late October of last year and included the planned timeframes for correcting security weaknesses. Agency corrective actions are underway, and while OMB indicated that performance in implementing these plans would be reflected in next year's report, information about the adequacy and reasonableness of such plans and the related costs to implement them, as well as an independent review, are important elements in congressional oversight and budget deliberations. In August 2001, OMB sent a memorandum to agency heads stating that it considered all reform provision material prepared by the CIOs for OMB to be predecisional and not releasable the public, the Congress, or GAO. In September, this subcommittee interceded to request that OMB provide the agency executive summaries to you, and OMB complied with this request. Recently, OMB agreed that it would also authorize the agencies to release the more detailed material to us after the agencies redact any sensitive information. OMB has continued to restrict access to agency corrective action plans. We plan to continue working with OMB in an effort to find workable solutions to obtain the information needed for congressional oversight. With the president requesting $4.2 billion for information security funding for fiscal year 2003, congressional oversight of future spending on information security will be important to ensuring that agencies are not using the funds they receive to continue ad hoc, piecemeal security fixes that are not supported by a strong agency risk management process. Accordingly, OMB should consider authorizing agencies to release appropriate information from the corrective action plans to the Congress. Also, future IG evaluations need to provide an independent assessment of agency corrective action plans.

- The report discusses review results for national security systems in several individual agency summaries, but does not summarize the overall results of the audits of the evaluations for these systems, which the reform provisions specifically require agencies to provide OMB and OMB to report subsequently to the Congress. This lack of an overall summary was compounded by limited access to information regarding national security systems by the director of central intelligence (DCI). The reform provisions assign the DCI and the secretary of defense specific responsibilities for national security systems, including developing and ensuring that information security policies, standards, and guidelines are implemented and designating the entity to perform the independent evaluation of the information security program and practices for these systems. As part of our review, DCI staff declined to meet with us to discuss the guidance and assistance they provided agencies to implement the reform provisions for national security systems. The DCI stated that our inquiry related to matters of intelligence oversight, which are under the purview of the congressional entities charged with overseeing the intelligence community. While evaluations and audits of evaluations for systems under the control of the DCI are available only to the appropriate oversight committees of Congress, OMB is required to report to the Congress on the results of audits of evaluations that the agencies submit to OMB for national security systems. We acknowledge the sensitivity of this information. Nevertheless, because the review, evaluation, and reporting requirements of the reform provisions apply to national security systems, as well as non-national-security systems, this lack of high-level summary information on implementation of the provisions and the security for national security systems limits the ability of the Congress to provide governmentwide oversight for information security. Consequently, we believe that OMB should consider providing appropriate information on national security systems to the Congress.

- OMB's report identifies lack of top management attention as a common weakness. It also notes that agencies have not implemented all the requirements of the legislation, and that it either disapproved or only conditionally approved the information security programs of each of the 24 agencies. However, the report does not address the status or effectiveness of the agencies' efforts to implement specific requirements of an agencywide information security program such as conducting risk assessments and testing and evaluating controls. OMB addresses these requirements in its individual agency summaries, but does not provide any overall results. Our analyses showed that most agencies have not fully implemented requirements to assess risk and test and evaluate controls and that this represents systemic weaknesses in the federal government's information security. Such requirements are critical elements of an overall information security program, and the Congress should be fully informed on the status of agency efforts to implement and comply with them. To address this, in its future annual reports to the Congress, OMB should consider explicitly identifying the overall status of agency efforts to implement each of the requirements for agency information security programs.

Reform Provisions Spur Agency Actions and Highlight Continued Weaknesses

To implement the reform provisions, agencies conducted management assessments of their information security programs and systems and followed OMB guidance to report their results. The methodologies that the agencies used varied, but most indicated that they used NIST's *Security Self-Assessment Guide* to assist program officials in reviewing their programs.[13] Provided to help agencies perform self-assessments of their information security programs and to accompany the NIST-developed *Federal IT Security Assessment Framework*,[14] this guide uses an extensive questionnaire containing specific control objectives and techniques against which an unclassified system or group of interconnected systems can be tested and measured. Most agencies considered this questionnaire to be a useful tool and several modified or tailored it for their use. In addition, several agencies used independent contractors to evaluate their systems, and in at least one case, an agency had its program assessed by the NIST Computer Security Expert Assist Team.[15]

In addition to these assessments of their information security programs, agencies also considered the results of audit work performed by their IGs, GAO, and others to help them identify information security weaknesses for reporting to OMB and identifying corrective actions. In particular, a number of agencies worked closely with the IGs to help ensure that they consistently identified weaknesses.

Most agencies structured their executive summaries according to the 13 topics that OMB's reporting instructions indicated they should address. However, these summaries did not always provide all requested data or provide context for determining the significance of their efforts. For example, they did not indicate the extent to which agency programs and

---

[13]National Institute of Standards and Technology *Security Self-Assessment Guide for Information Technology Systems*, NIST Special Publication 800-26, November 2001.

[14]National Institute of Standards and Technology, *Federal Information Technology Security Assessment Framework*, prepared for the Federal CIO Council by the NIST Computer Security Division Systems and Network Security Group, November 28, 2000.

[15]NIST created the Computer Security Expert Assist Team (CSEAT) to improve federal critical infrastructure protection planning and implementation efforts by assisting governmental entities in improving the security of their information and cyber assets. The CSEAT review of an agency's computer security program is based on a combination of proven techniques and best practices and results in an action plan that provides a federal agency with a business-case-based roadmap to cost-effectively enhance the protection of their information system assets.

systems, contractor-supported operations, or national security system programs were covered by their review.

In general, our analyses of these summaries showed that although agencies are making progress in addressing information security, much remains to be done. None of the agencies had fully implemented the requirements of the reform provisions and all continue to have significant information security weaknesses. In particular, we identified the following key information security requirements of the reform provisions that were problematic for the 24 agencies reviewed.

Extent that Agencies Assess Risk is Unknown

The reform provisions require agencies to perform periodic threat-based risk assessments for systems and data. However, the agency and IG reports indicated that most agencies could not demonstrate that periodic risk assessments are being conducted. However, none of the 24 agencies had conducted risk assessments for all their systems, and 11, or 46 percent, had not established effective performance measures to show how well program officials met these requirements.

Risk assessments are an essential element of risk management and overall security program management and, as our best practice work has shown,[16] are an integral part of the management processes of leading organizations. Risk assessments help ensure that the greatest risks have been identified and addressed, increase the understanding of risk, and provide support for needed controls. Our reviews of federal agencies, however, frequently show deficiencies related to assessing risk, such as security plans for major systems that are not developed based on risks. As a result, the agencies had accepted an unknown level of risk by default rather than consciously deciding what level of risk was tolerable.

OMB reporting guidance addressed this requirement by asking agencies to describe performance measures used to ensure that agency program officials have assessed the risk to operations and assets under their control. In its report to the Congress, OMB identified measuring performance as a common weakness and covered risk assessments in its individual agency summaries. OMB did not, however, identify the

---

[16]GAO/AIMD-98-68, May 1998.

pervasive lack of risk assessments as an overall weakness in federal information security.

Policies and Procedures Not Adequate

The reform provisions require agencies to establish information security policies and procedures that are commensurate with risk and that comprehensively address the other reform provisions. OMB's report refers to selected policies and procedures, but does not address them comprehensively. Because risks are not adequately assessed, policies and procedures may be inadequate or excessive. Also, our audits have identified instances where agency policies and procedures did not comprehensively address all areas of security, were not sufficiently detailed, were outdated, or were inconsistent across the agency.

Security Training and Awareness Efforts Incomplete

The reform provisions require agencies to provide training on security responsibilities for information security personnel and on security awareness for agency personnel. Agency summaries showed that some agencies provided little or no training, and many could not show to what extent security training was provided. For example, 4 of the 24 agencies (17 percent) reported that they were still developing or implementing their security awareness and training program. Further, 10 of the 24 agencies (42 percent) did not report data to indicate the number of agency employees receiving security training, and 8 (33 percent) did not report the total costs of providing such training.

Our studies of best practices at leading organizations have shown that these organizations took steps to ensure that personnel involved in various aspects of their information security programs had the skills and knowledge they needed.[17] They also recognized that staff expertise had to be frequently updated to keep abreast of ongoing changes in threats, vulnerabilities, software, security techniques, and security monitoring tools. In addition, our past information security reviews at individual agencies have shown that they have not provided adequate computer security training to their employees including contractor staff.

In its report to the Congress, OMB identified security education and awareness as a common weakness and noted that OMB and federal

---

[17]GAO/AIMD-98-68. May 1998.

agencies are now working through the new Critical Infrastructure
Protection Board's education committee and the CIO Council's Workforce
Committee to address this issue. Also, the CIO Council's Best Practices
Committee is working with NIST through NIST's Federal Agency Security
Practices Website to identify and disseminate best practices involving
security training. Finally, OMB notes that one of the administration's
electronic government initiatives is to establish and deliver electronic
training.

Security Controls Not Adequately Tested and Evaluated

Under the reform provisions, one of the responsibilities of the agency head
is to ensure that appropriate agency officials are responsible for
periodically testing and evaluating the effectiveness of policies,
procedures, controls, and techniques. Many of the 24 agencies we
contacted said that they primarily relied on management self-assessments
to review their programs or systems this first year and did not perform any
control testing as part of these assessments. Several agencies indicated
that control testing was part of their certification and accreditation
processes, but also reported that many systems were not certified and
accredited.[18]

Periodically evaluating the effectiveness of security policies and controls
and acting to address any identified weaknesses are fundamental activities
that allow an organization to manage its information security risks cost
effectively, rather than reacting to individual problems ad hoc only after a
violation has been detected or an audit finding has been reported. Further,
management control testing and evaluation as part of the program reviews
can supplement control testing and evaluation in IG and GAO audits to
help provide a more complete picture of the agencies' security postures.

OMB's report to the Congress also did not specifically identify lack of
control testing as a common weakness, but did address it as part of the
individual agency summaries.

---

[18]Certification is a formal review and test of a system's security safeguards to determine
whether or not they meet security needs and applicable requirements. Accreditation is the
formal authorization for system operation and is usually supported by certification of the
system's security safeguards, including its management, operational, and technical
controls.

Remedial Actions May Not be Adequate

The reform provisions require that agencies develop a process for ensuring that remedial action is taken to address significant deficiencies. While we were unable to review the adequacy of corrective action plans submitted to OMB, our audits have identified instances in which items on other agency corrective action plans were not independently verified or considered with respect to other systems that might contain the same or similar weakness. We have also noted instances where agencies had no process to accumulate identified deficiencies across the agency. Given these prior findings, it is important that corrective action plans be carefully reviewed.

Incident-Handling and Information-Sharing Procedures Not Implemented

The reform provisions require agencies to implement procedures for detecting, reporting, and responding to security incidents. Of the 24 agencies we reviewed, 18 (75 percent) reported that they had documented incident handling procedures, but had not implemented these procedures agencywide. In addition, 5 agencies (22 percent) reported that their procedures did not cover reporting incidents to the Federal Computer Incident Response Center (FedCIRC)[19] or law enforcement.

Even strong controls may not block all intrusions and misuse, but organizations can reduce the risks associated with such events if they promptly take steps to detect intrusions and misuse before significant damage can be done. In addition, accounting for and analyzing security problems and incidents are effective ways for an organization to gain a better understanding of threats to its information and of the cost of its security-related problems. Such analyses can also pinpoint vulnerabilities that need to be addressed to help ensure that they will not be exploited again. In this regard, problem and incident reports can provide valuable input for risk assessments, help in prioritizing security improvement efforts, and be used to illustrate risks and related trends in reports to senior management.

Our information security reviews also confirm that federal agencies have not adequately (1) prevented intrusions before they occur, (2) detected intrusions as they occur, (3) responded to successful intrusions, or (4)

---

[19]GSA's FedCIRC provides a central focal point for incident reporting, handling, prevention and recognition for the federal government. Its purpose is to ensure that the government has critical services available in order to withstand or quickly recover from attacks against its information resources.

reported intrusions to staff and management. Such weaknesses provide little assurance that unauthorized attempts to access sensitive information will be identified and appropriate actions taken in time to prevent or minimize damage.

In its report to the Congress, OMB identified "detecting, reporting, and sharing information on vulnerabilities" as a common agency weakness. It also noted that ongoing activity to address this issue includes FedCIRC's quarterly reporting to OMB on the federal government's status on security incidents and GSA's, under OMB and Critical Infrastructure Protection Board guidance, exploring of methods to disseminate vulnerability patches to all agencies more effectively.

Critical Assets Identified, But Not Ranked

The reform provisions require that each agencywide information security program ensure the integrity, confidentiality, and availability of systems and data supporting the agency's critical operations and assets. Of the 24 agencies covered by our review, 15 had not implemented an effective methodology such as Project Matrix reviews[20] to identify their critical assets, and 7 had not determined the priority for restoring these assets should a disruption in critical operations occur.

At many of the agencies we have reviewed, we found incomplete plans and procedures to ensure that critical operations can continue when unexpected events occur, such as a temporary power failure, accidental loss of files, or a major disaster. These plans and procedures are incomplete because operations and supporting resources had not been fully analyzed to determine which were most critical and would need to be restored first. Further, existing plans were not fully tested to identify their weaknesses. As a result, many agencies have inadequate assurance that they can recover operational capability in a timely, orderly manner after a disruptive attack.

OMB's report to the Congress does not specifically address the overall extent to which agencies identified and prioritized their critical assets, but does cover this topic in the individual agency summaries. Also, OMB

---

[20]The Department of Commerce's Critical Infrastructure Assurance Office established Project Matrix to provide a standard methodology for identifying all assets, nodes, networks, and associated infrastructure dependencies and interdependencies required for the federal government to fulfill its national security, economic stability, and critical public health and safety responsibilities to the American people.

indicates that it will direct all large agencies to undertake a Project Matrix review, and once these reviews are completed, it will identify cross-government activities and lines of business for Matrix reviews.

Agency Efforts to Ensure Security of Contractor-Provided Services are Limited

Under the reform provisions, agencies are required to develop and implement risk-based, cost-effective policies and procedures to provide security protections for information collected or maintained either by the agency or for it by another agency or contractor. Laws and policies have included security requirements for years, but agency reports indicate that although most included security requirements in their service contracts, most not did they have a process to ensure the security of services provided by a contractor or another agency.

OMB reported this as a common weakness in its report to the Congress noting that activities to address this issue include (1) working under the guidance of an OMB-led security committee established under Executive Order 13231 to develop recommendations addressing security in contracts themselves,[21] and (2) working with the CIO Council and the Procurement Executives Council to establish a training program that ensures appropriate security training for contractors.

Agencies May Not Identify All Significant Security Weaknesses

The reform provisions require agencies to examine the adequacy and effectiveness of information security policies, procedures, and practices, and to report any significant deficiency found as a material weakness under the applicable criteria for other laws, including the Clinger-Cohen Act of 1996, the Chief Financial Officers Act of 1990, and the Federal Managers Financial Integrity Act. Although most agencies reported security weaknesses, several did not identify all weaknesses highlighted in the IGs' independent evaluations. For example, two IGs identified security weaknesses, but the CIOs did not identify any weaknesses in their executive summaries because they were not considered material weaknesses.

As I will illustrate next in my discussion of the results of the IGs' independent evaluations, our latest analyses of audit results for the 24 agencies confirmed that all agencies had significant information security

---

[21] "Critical Infrastructure Protection in the Information Age," Executive Order 13231, October 16, 2001.

GAO-02-470T

weaknesses. Such weaknesses should be identified and reported in the CIOs' reports consistent with the IGs' independent evaluations to ensure that they are appropriately considered in implementing corrective actions.

IG Role Critical to Agency Implementation and Reporting

The reform provisions assign the agency IGs a critical role in the overall implementation and reporting process. Each agency is to have the IG or other independent evaluator annually evaluate its information security program and practices. This evaluation is to include testing of the effectiveness of information security control techniques for an appropriate subset of the agency's information systems and an assessment of the agency's compliance with the legislation; it may also use existing audits, evaluations, or reports relating to the programs or practices of the agency. For national security systems, the secretary of defense or DCI designates who is to perform the independent evaluation, but the IG is to perform an audit of the evaluation. The results of each evaluation of non-national-security systems and of the audit of the evaluation for national security systems are to be reported to OMB.

Individually, as well as collectively, the annual independent evaluations provide much needed information for improved oversight by OMB and the Congress. Our years of auditing agency security programs have shown that independent tests and evaluations are essential to verifying the effectiveness of computer-based controls. The independent evaluations can also evaluate agency implementation of management initiatives, thus promoting management accountability. Moreover, an annual independent evaluation of agency information security programs will help drive reform because it will spotlight both the obstacles and progress toward improving information security.

For this first-year evaluation and reporting for the reform provisions, IGs primarily performed the independent evaluations and largely relied on existing or ongoing work to evaluate agency security, most of which was related to their financial statement audits. With the reform provisions applicable to essentially all major systems including national security systems, as well as other types of risk beyond financial statements, future IG independent evaluation efforts will have to expand their coverage to include such additional risks and more nonfinancial systems, particularly for agencies with significant nonfinancial operations such as the departments of Defense and Justice. An important step toward ensuring information security is to fully understand the weaknesses that exist, and as the body of audit evidence expands, it is probable that additional significant deficiencies will be identified. However, this expanded coverage will also place a significant new burden on existing audit capabilities, which will require ensuring that agency IGs have sufficient resources to either perform or contract for the needed work.

While no format was prescribed for their evaluation reports, most IGs prepared an executive summary and report which, at OMB's request, addressed the specific topics identified in OMB's reporting guidance. This made comparison of agency and IG results easier, and better highlighted discrepancies. For the most part and particularly where the CIO and IG offices coordinated their responses, the IG evaluations were consistent with what the agencies reported. However, there were areas where the CIO reviews and the IG evaluations did not agree in their assessments of the agencies' progress in implementing the requirements of the reform provisions. Reasons cited include different interpretations of the law or guidance and the time lag between the audit reports the IG used for its evaluation and the possibly more current status reflected in the CIO's review.

However, perhaps the most important area of the IGs' independent evaluations is their identification of the agency's significant information security weaknesses for which they identified essentially known weaknesses including, but not limited to, those considered material weaknesses under reporting requirements for other legislation. To summarize these identified weaknesses, we also analyzed the results of IG and GAO audit reports published from July 2000 through September 2001, including the results of the IGs' independent evaluations. These analyses showed significant information security weaknesses in all major areas of the agencies' general controls—the policies, procedures, and technical controls that apply to all or a large segment of an entity's information systems and help ensure their proper operation. Figure 1 illustrates the distribution of weaknesses across the 24 agencies for the following six general control areas: (1) security program management, which provides the framework for ensuring that risks are understood and that effective controls are selected and properly implemented; (2) access controls, which ensure that only authorized individuals can read, alter, or delete data; (3) software development and change controls, which ensure that only authorized software programs are implemented; (4) segregation of duties, which reduces the risk that one individual can independently perform inappropriate actions without detection; (5) operating systems controls, which protect sensitive programs that support multiple applications from tampering and misuse; and (6) service continuity, which ensures that computer-dependent operations experience no significant disruptions.

Figure 1: Information Security Weaknesses at 24 Major Agencies

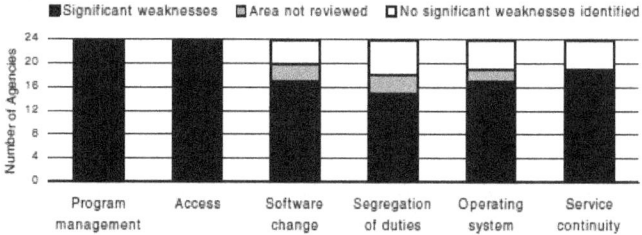

Source: Audit reports issued July 2000 through September 2001.

Our analysis shows that weaknesses were most often identified for security program management, access controls, and service continuity controls. For security program management, we found weaknesses for all 24 agencies in 2001 as compared to 21 agencies (88 percent) in a similar analysis in 2000.[22] For access controls, we also found weaknesses for all 24 agencies in 2001—the same condition we found in 2000. For service continuity controls, we found weaknesses at 19 of the 24 agencies (79 percent) as compared to 20 agencies or 83 percent in 2000.

Reform Provisions Create Agency and IG Challenges

Agencies identified challenges during their first-year implementation of the reform provisions, some of which, according to the agencies, limited the extent of their efforts. Perhaps most significantly, several agencies acknowledged that they had not been reviewing their systems according to existing requirements in OMB Circular A-130. As a result, they did not have system reviews they could use to help respond to review requirements of the reform provisions. In addition, several agencies sought contractor assistance, but said that delays in obtaining this help limited what they could do in time to meet the September 10 deadline for reporting to OMB.

---

[22]U.S. General Accounting Office, *Computer Security: Critical Federal Operations and Assets Remain at Risk.* GAO/T-AIMD-00-314. Washington, D.C.: September 11, 2000.

For example, one agency was still trying to obtain contractor services as late as July 2001 with the reporting deadline only 2 months away. Also, several agencies noted that late final guidance from OMB on reporting also limited what they could do to gather and report information. Many agencies also had not maintained data that OMB requested be reported, such as training statistics and actual performance measure results that would help them demonstrate the extent to which they had met security requirements.

One final challenge emphasized by many agencies was the need for adequate funding to implement security requirements. Several agencies noted that funding limitations had directly affected their ability to implement existing security requirements and, thus, affected their compliance with the reform provisions. Although, in most instances, this issue involved a lack of funding, in at least one agency, CIO staff pointed to specific security funding the agency received as key to the improvement efforts it has undertaken in recent years.

While citing funding as an implementation challenge, agencies apparently had difficulty identifying how much they spend related to information security. The security costs that OMB requested agencies to report were not provided in some cases. In addition, for costs that were provided, there was no detail as to what these costs consisted of or how they are actually reflected in agency budget submissions. Further, while most of the 24 agencies we reviewed reported that they had integrated security into their capital planning and investment control process, 19 (79 percent) reported that they had not included security requirements and costs on every fiscal year 2002 capital asset plan submitted to OMB.

In addition to incomplete security cost data, costs that were reported to OMB varied widely. On the basis of the final costs shown in OMB's report to the Congress, we present, in figure 2, the 24 agencies' fiscal year 2002 security funding as a percentage of their total information technology spending. These percentages range from a high of 17.0 percent for the Department of Labor to a low of 1.0 percent for the Department of Agriculture.

Figure 2: Percentage of Agency Fiscal Year 2002 Information Technology (IT)
Budget Allocated to IT Security

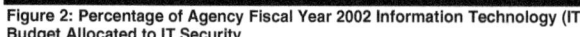
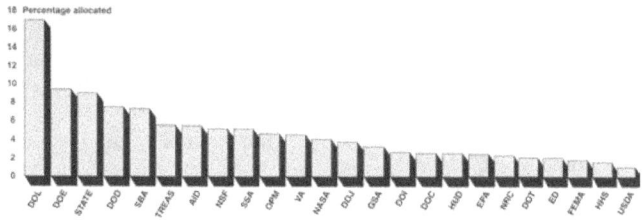

18 Percentage allocated

24 federal CFO agencies

OMB reports that it assessed the agencies' performance against the
amount they spent and did not find that increased security spending equals
increased security performance. As a result, it concludes that there is no
evidence that poor security is a result of lack of money, and that
improvements in security performance will come from agencies giving
significant attention to the security weaknesses it describes in its report.

While security funding might not always correlate with security
performance, information security does involve costs, and OMB
acknowledges the importance of this funding by requiring agencies to
identify security funding in their budget submissions. We also agree with
OMB that much can be done to cost-effectively address common
weaknesses, such as security training, across government rather than
piecemeal by agency. At the same time, however, agencies have specific
weaknesses that they must correct. OMB has required agencies to identify
these weaknesses and to indicate the level of resources required to correct
them in their corrective action plans.

From the IGs' perspective, several have indicated that the requirement for
an annual evaluation will represent a challenge because of their difficulty
in obtaining adequate resources in today's competitive market for
information security professionals. Further, by conducting an evaluation
every year, these IGs believe they will lose the ability to deploy current
limited resources in other important areas and may have to limit the scope
of their work.

Page 28   GAO-02-470T

Improvement Efforts are Underway, But Challenges to Federal Information Security Remain

As I discussed previously, a number of improvement efforts have been undertaken in the past few years both at an agency and governmentwide level. Among these efforts and partially in response to the events of September 11, 2001, the president created the Office of Homeland Security, with duties that include coordinating efforts to protect critical public and private information systems within the United States from terrorist attack. The president also (1) appointed a special advisor for cyberspace security to coordinate interagency efforts to secure information systems and (2) created the President's Critical Infrastructure Protection Board to recommend policies and coordinate programs for protecting information for critical infrastructure. The board is to include a standing committee for executive branch information systems security, chaired by an OMB designee.

These actions are laudable. However, given recent events and reports that critical operations and assets continue to be highly vulnerable to computer-based attacks, the government still faces a challenge in ensuring that risks from cyber threats are appropriately addressed in the context of the broader array of risks to the nation's welfare. Accordingly, it is important that federal information security efforts be guided by a comprehensive strategy for improvement. In 1998, shortly after the initial issuance of Presidential Decision Directive (PDD) 63 on protecting the nation's critical infrastructure, we recommended that OMB, which, by law, is responsible for overseeing federal information security, and the assistant to the president for national security affairs work together to ensure that the roles of new and existing federal efforts were coordinated under a comprehensive strategy.[23] Our more recent reviews of the National Infrastructure Protection Center and of broader federal efforts to counter computer-based attacks showed that there was a continuing need to clarify responsibilities and critical infrastructure protection objectives.[24] As the administration refines the strategy that it has begun to lay out in recent months, it is imperative that it takes steps to ensure that information security receives appropriate attention and resources and that known deficiencies are addressed.

---

[23]U.S. General Accounting Office, *Information Security: Serious Weaknesses Place Critical Federal Operations and Assets at Risk.* GAO/AIMD-98-92. Washington, D.C.: September 23, 1998.

[24]U.S. General Accounting Office, *Critical Infrastructure Protection: Significant Challenges in Developing National Capabilities.* GAO-01-323. Washington, D.C.: April 25, 2001; *Combating Terrorism: Selected Challenges and Related Recommendations.* GAO-01-822. Washington, D.C.: September 20, 2001.

First, it is important that the federal strategy delineate the roles and responsibilities of the numerous entities involved in federal information security and related aspects of critical infrastructure protection. Under current law, OMB is responsible for overseeing and coordinating federal agency security, and NIST, with assistance from the National Security Agency, is responsible for establishing related standards. In addition, interagency bodies—such as the CIO Council and the entities created under PDD 63 on critical infrastructure protection—are attempting to coordinate agency initiatives. Although these organizations have developed fundamentally sound policies and guidance and have undertaken potentially useful initiatives, effective improvements are not yet taking place. Further, it is unclear how the activities of these many organizations interrelate, who should be held accountable for their success or failure, and whether they will effectively and efficiently support national goals.

Second, more specific guidance to agencies on the controls that they need to implement could help ensure adequate protection. Currently, agencies have wide discretion in deciding what computer security controls to implement and the level of rigor with which to enforce these controls. In theory, this discretion is appropriate since, as OMB and NIST guidance states, the level of protection that agencies provide should be commensurate with the risk to agency operations and assets. In essence, one set of specific controls will not be appropriate for all types of systems and data. Nevertheless, our studies of best practices at leading organizations have shown that more specific guidance is important.[25] In particular, specific mandatory standards for varying risk levels can clarify expectations for information protection, including audit criteria; provide a standard framework for assessing information security risk; help ensure that shared data are appropriately protected; and reduce demands for limited resources to independently develop security controls. Implementing such standards for federal agencies would require developing a single set of information classification categories for use by all agencies to define the criticality and sensitivity of the various types of information they maintain. It would also necessitate establishing minimum mandatory requirements for protecting information in each classification category.

---

[25]GAO/AIMD-98-68, May 1998.

Third, ensuring effective implementation of agency information security and critical infrastructure protection plans will require active monitoring by the agencies to determine if milestones are being met and testing to determine if policies and controls are operating as intended. Routine periodic audits, such as those required by the reform provisions, would allow for more meaningful performance measurement. In addition, the annual evaluation, reporting, and monitoring process established through these provisions, is an important mechanism, previously missing, to hold agencies accountable for implementing effective security and to manage the problem from a governmentwide perspective.

Fourth, the Congress and the executive branch can use audit results to monitor agency performance and take whatever action is deemed advisable to remedy identified problems. Such oversight is essential for holding agencies accountable for their performance, as was demonstrated by the OMB and congressional efforts to oversee the Year 2000 computer challenge.

Fifth, agencies must have the technical expertise they need to select, implement, and maintain controls that protect their information systems. Similarly, the federal government must maximize the value of its technical staff by sharing expertise and information. Highlighted during the Year 2000 challenge, the availability of adequate technical and audit expertise is a continuing concern to agencies.

Sixth, agencies can allocate resources sufficient to support their information security and infrastructure protection activities. Funding for security is already embedded to some extent in agency budgets for computer system development efforts and routine network and system management and maintenance. However, some additional amounts are likely to be needed to address specific weaknesses and new tasks. OMB and congressional oversight of future spending on information security will be important to ensuring that agencies are not using the funds they receive to continue ad hoc, piecemeal security fixes that are not supported by a strong agency risk management process.

Seventh, expanded research is needed in the area of information systems protection. While a number of research efforts are underway, experts have noted that more is needed to achieve significant advances. As the director of the CERT® Coordination Center testified before this subcommittee last September, "It is essential to seek fundamental technological solutions and to seek proactive, preventive approaches, not just reactive, curative approaches." In addition, in its December 2001 third annual report, the Advisory Panel to Assess Domestic Response Capabilities for Terrorism Involving Weapons of Mass Destruction (also known as the Gilmore Commission) recommended that the Office of Homeland Security develop and implement a comprehensive plan for research, development, test, and evaluation to enhance cyber security.[26]

In summary, first-year implementation of the reform provisions has resulted in a number of positive initiatives and benefits, and OMB, the agencies, and the IGs all undertook efforts to implement these provisions. However, faced with limited past efforts to implement security and other obstacles, agencies in their reviews did not provide the scope or depth of coverage intended, particularly in testing and evaluating controls. The IGs also had to rely primarily on their existing work for this first-year effort. Consequently, much work remains to be done to achieve the objectives of the reform legislation. In addition, OMB did not report to the Congress on key elements of the provisions, such as the adequacy of agencies' corrective action plans and overall evaluation results for national security systems, or provide supporting information. We plan to continue to work with OMB in an effort to find workable solutions to obtain the information needed for congressional oversight. These factors limit congressional insight into the status of information security for the federal government, as well as its ability to perform its responsibilities for oversight and budget deliberations. Further, with the increasing threat to critical federal operations and assets and poor federal information security, as indicated by reform provision reviews and evaluations, it is imperative that the administration and the agencies implement a comprehensive strategy for improvement that emphasizes information security and addresses known weaknesses.

Mr. Chairman, this concludes my statement. I would be pleased to answer any questions that you or other members of the Subcommittee may have at this time.

---

[26] *Third Annual Report to the President and Congress of the Advisory Panel to Assess Domestic Response Capabilities for Terrorism Involving Weapons of Mass Destruction.* December 15, 2001.

Page 32   GAO-02-470T

Contact

If you should have any questions about the testimony, please contact me at (202) 512-3317. I can be reached by e-mail at *daceyr@gao.gov*.

(310151)

GAO-02-470T

GAO Contact and Staff Acknowledgments

GAO Contact	Ben Ritt, (202) 512-6443
Acknowledgments	In addition to the person named above, Ronald Beers, Justin Booth, Jean Boltz, Debra Conner, Larry Crosland, Kirk Daubenspeck, Patrick Dugan, Sophia Harrison, Danielle Hollomon, David Irvin, Carol Langelier, Paula Moore, Freda Paintsil, Ronald Parker, Crawford Thompson, William Thompson, Rosanna Villa, Charles Vrabel, William Wadsworth, and Gregory Wilshusen made key contributions to this report.

PRINTED ON RECYCLED PAPER